Such Is Life

Maya Williams

BookLeaf
Publishing

India | USA | UK

Presentation by *BookLeaf Publishing*

Web: www.bookleafpub.com

E-mail: info@bookleafpub.com

ISBN: 9789360940850

First edition 2024

The future

ACKNOWLEDGEMENT

Humans

PREFACE

Sometimes we get it, sometimes we don't.

Stuck on maybe.

Like a garden unable to soak up the rain of your affection, I remain parched, a desert yearning for your love to be my oasis. We are two stars in separate galaxies, unable to embrace the celestial dance that would forge an unbreakable bond. The waiting has cast shadows on my heart, revealing that love cannot be handpicked like ripe fruit from a tree. The empty spaces of uncertainty cannot be filled with wishful thinking. The "I miss you" echoes do not reverberate through every passing day of your absence, nor does the phrase "I love you" resonate with every beat of my existence. The promise of your return is not simply the arrival of the next weekend, nor is it the moment you step away from your daily grind.

A locked gaze is not a tome of unspoken confessions; it is simply the revelation of presence, a fleeting glimpse of reality, not a pause in the relentless march of time. Perhaps does not equate to acquiescence; it stands at the crossroads of certainty and doubt, a bridge between what is and what could be. Our narrative meanders between the starkness of truth and the buoyancy of aspirations, uncertain whether our tale will ever find its harmonious cadence.

One day, the notion of love that I hold may not always be at the forefront, eagerly awaiting your arrival. One day, my armor will shield me from my own vulnerabilities until that moment arrives, I find myself caught in the endless cycle of " he loves me" and "he loves me not."

Echoes of Love and Reflections of Self

How many "I love you"s have you heard?
How many of them did you need to believe?
How many hearts have you broken?
How many hearts did you hide from, to keep
from turning rotten,
Because you know they were pure, but your
presence was only temporary,
So you could fill yours up again.

How many have forgiven you,
And how many have lost trust in men because of
you?
Are you a victim or a villain in your own story,
Or are you trying to perpetuate the idea out loud
that you are trying to find your purpose?

How many times have you apologized to one,
But restarted the same pattern with another?
Am I a fool or a hopeless romantic?
You once said, "our timing is always off",
I've been trying to figure out if this is a waste of
time,
Or am I lost, trying to be in the same time zone
as you?

What if my heartbeats are just the strokes of
time waiting for you?

I've been around for several seasons,
Showing up the same through each change with
perfect timing,
And now it seems as if global warming is
catching up to me,
Because you haven't learned to nurture love in
its purity.
So the pollution and all the toxins are causing
changes in my natural element of loving you.
Guess I'm becoming corrosion,
Fragile sediments settling at the bottom of the
ocean,
Trying to keep my head above water, saving the
love I have left for you.

In doing so, I caught my reflection, and it asked,
"Hey girl, who's gonna save you?"
Doing all this thinking and forgot I wanna be
loved too.

GANELL

You're a rare and precious bloom,
A radiant sunbeam piercing through the gloom.
Your laughter, a melody that dances on the wind,
Your spirit, a river that knows no end.

Like a sturdy oak, you weather every storm,
Your strength and grace, a symphony in form.
In the fabric of friendships, you're a vibrant
thread,
Unyielding, undaunted, by the words left unsaid.

Your smile, a beacon in the darkest night,
A constellation of hope, burning ever bright.
Your eyes, two pools of wisdom and grace,
Reflecting the beauty of your resilient embrace.

Though the road may twist and the path grow
steep,
Your spirit soars high, never confined to the
deep.
You're a warrior, a champion, a force to behold,
A phoenix rising, as stories of courage are told.
Cause my oh my do you have some!
So let's raise a glass to the journey you tread,
To the love, the laughter, the tears you've shed.

For in every heartbeat, in every breath you take,
You're a masterpiece of life, an enduring,
unyielding wake.

In the realm of fashion, you're a true trendsetter,
Your style a work of art, each outfit better and
better.
With an eye for elegance, you effortlessly shine,
A runway of grace, a fashionista so fine.

Your love for shoes, a collection so divine,
Each pair a masterpiece, a story to enshrine.
From stilettos to sneakers, you wear them with
flair,
A reflection of your spirit, bold and debonair.

In the dance of life, you're the belle of the ball,
Your elegance and poise, captivating all.
Your love for beauty, a tapestry so grand,
A portrait of sophistication, a brushstroke so
grand.

So here's to you, my friend, in every way
supreme,
A beacon of strength, a radiant, resplendent
dream.
In love, in fashion, in all that you pursue,
You're top tier, unparalleled, forever shining
true.

Don't let your kids try you.

Dear daughter, a precious seed I've sown,
Your life, a winding river all your own,
Each breath, a gentle breeze you breathe,
Each step, a dance, a rhythm you lead.

Your dreams, a flock of birds taking flight,
Your joy, a radiant sun shining bright,
Your pain, a storm that may pass through,
Your honor, a flame that guides you true.

In trials and tribulations, you find strength,
Your self-esteem, a mirror of infinite length,
Your flaws, mere shadows in your light,
Your journey, a quilt stitched with care.

Your destination, a star you'll reach,
Your rights, a crown no one can breach,
Your wrongs, lessons in disguise,
All these, beneath your watchful eyes.

As you navigate this world's grand stage,
I am your compass, your guiding sage,
The director of your play, unseen,
The law keeper in your inner scene.

I am the protector, the shield you hold,
The warrior in stories yet untold,
The bigger voice in times of doubt,
The comfort zone when fears sprout.

But remember, dear child, in this grand ballet,
I am not one to be led astray,
For you are mine, a part of me,
And my roots run deep, through eternity.

You are not my flaw, nor my burden to bear,
In flaws of mine, a cure we share,
A moment of silence, a step back in time,
A reflective reset, a prayer sublime.

You can be a season, fleeting and bright,
Or a root, grounding me in the night,
Yet I am the tree, strong and true,
Unbowed by shadows that may accrue.

You are not overlooked, you are my muse,
Spoken into existence, you'll never lose,
They say I'm raising you well, with care,
In healthy gardens, we make a pair.

But if my roots strain, trying to save,
Branches that refuse to behave,
Insisting on paths that lead astray,
I'll disconnect, find a different way.

For my emotional health, a sacred space,
No darkness in your light I'll embrace,
Your soil well-tended, through every season,
No cloud shall dim your inner beacon.

So stand tall, my daughter, in your grace,
In the garden of life, find your place,
For you are a treasure, beyond compare,
A bloom so rare, in the open air.

Love and letting go

In the dance of life and love,
I welcomed you back like a dove,
Hoping this time you'd see,
The depths of love inside of me.

Maybe you finally realized,
That our bond wasn't disguised,
Our silent hugs spoke loud and clear,
Of a connection so sincere.

I thought you saw I was your one,
Your safe harbor in the stormy run,
But deep down, I knew the truth,
Your return was a cloak for your uncouth.

Life's boulders weighed heavy on your soul,
Seeking solace in my gentle hold,
Five years apart did not erase,
The patterns of your transient grace.

I wanted to believe in a different tale,
But the voice inside me couldn't fail,
To see through your charade,
Of using me as a temporary aid.

No longer the girl you once knew,
I stand as a woman, strong and true,
A mother, a recipient of a broken heart,
No longer willing to play my old part.

I'll no longer let you slip away,
Silent and unchallenged in your play,
Deserving of respect, I demand,
No longer willing to hold your hand.

You returned with the same old game,
But this time, I won't be tame,
Calling out each move you make,
No longer willing to partake.

Was I not deserving of your truth?
Or was I just a folly in your youth?
Better to hear the painful real,
Than to live in a lie's tight seal.

Breath of resilience

In the rhythm of life, we all breathe,
A dance of existence, a whisper beneath.
When the breath becomes a tale told,
I sense the weight, the burdens unfold.

Time whispers softly, "Slow down, dear one,
Take a deep breath, let the chaos be undone."
Amidst the storm, I seek a tranquil shore,
To recenter my soul, to breathe in once more.

In the symphony of my breath's rise and fall,
I uncover the moments, big and small.
Grateful for the now, hopeful for the morrow,
Embracing the joy, dismissing the sorrow.

Life's battles may rage, fierce and wild,
Yet in the pause, peace reconciled.
Saying no amidst the clamor's roar,
To stand alone, to fight for more.

Not every battle can be mine to fight,
Some paths must be walked in the night.
Cheering silently, from afar I send,
Strength and love, until the very end.

Just as in breathing, in victory we find,
A resilience deep, in the human kind.
For as long as breath fills our chest,
In every trial, we find our best.

Intuition speaks

In the deep well of the soul, a whispering wind,
Intuition dances, a flame that will never rescind.
An ancient compass, a guide unseen,
Like a mystical forest, where shadows convene.

It's a spark in the dark, a flickering light,
A cosmic river flowing, beyond human sight.
Intuition is a silent symphony, a song of the
heart,
A painter's palette, where colors never depart.

Like a bird in flight, soaring high and free,
Or a sailor at sea, guided by a distant decree.
It's a shimmering star, in the vast night sky,
A hidden treasure, waiting to mystify.

Intuition is the moon, pulling the tides,
A secret language, where truth always abides.
Like a blooming flower, in the still of the night,
Or a shooting star, blazing with celestial might.

Listen closely to the whispers, the subtle cues,
Intuition is the energy that guides and imbues.
Trust in its wisdom, let it be your song,
For intuition knows where you truly belong.

God, are you there?

15

God's heartbeat steady,
Echoes of faith and love guide
Through life's winding paths

Broken dreams

In the realm of shattered dreams, where hopes
once soared,
Lies a landscape of broken promises, where
dreams are ignored.
Whispers of what could have been, echo in the
night,
Fading visions of the past, lost in the fading
light.

Like a fragile glass sculpture, dreams lie in
ruins,
Scattered pieces of ambition, like forgotten
tunes.
The fabric of imaginings, now torn and frayed,
In the shadows of broken dreams, we find where
we've strayed.

Paths once paved with golden dreams, now
overgrown with doubt,
Lost in the labyrinth of broken dreams, we try to
find a way out.
Yet in the debris of shattered hopes, new seeds
may sow,
From the ashes of broken dreams, new
aspirations grow.

So let us not be defined by the dreams that lie
shattered,
But by the resilience to rise again, nothing else
mattered.
In the jigsaw of broken dreams, we find strength
anew,
For in the dance of life's uncertainties, dreams
are born afresh and true.

That 9-5

In the grind of nine to five, we toil away,
Chasing bills, the rent we must pay.
Dreams deferred, set aside for now,
Surviving somehow, but not sure how.

The clock ticks on, each passing day,
A cycle of work, a price to pay.
Not the dream job we long to find,
Yet it's the reality we must bind.

A roof over head, a basic need,
In this world of hustle and greed.
The daily grind, the endless race,
Searching for a better place.

Not all can have the finest slice,
Sometimes we settle for what will suffice.
Working hard, hoping someday we'll see,
A brighter future, where we can be free.

So we push through, with strength and might,
Facing each day, embracing the fight.
For in the struggle, we find our worth,
As we navigate this journey on earth.

Whispers in the rain

In the land where dreams once soared,
Hope's tender spark now wanes,
A weary heart no longer floored,
By visions that time restrains.

The Greater Good, a distant haze,
Shrouded in a veil of doubt,
A skeptic's gaze, a silent craze,
As faith gives way to a muted shout.

Each day unfolds in shades of gray,
A steady rain, a ceaseless fall,
Embracing chaos in its own way,
Accepting fate, surrendering all.

No longer seeking grand design,
In the symphony of life's refrain,
Just a soul adrift, a quiet sign,
Content to endure the endless rain.

The storm within, a gentle thrum,
A lullaby of sorrow's grace,
Finding solace in the constant drum,
Of tears that fall upon this place.

So let the tempest rage and roar,
For in its midst, a peace is found,
A whispered truth, a hidden lore,
In acceptance, in the rain unbound.

And though the Greater Good may fade,
In the shadowed depths of doubt,
A quiet strength is gently made,
In embracing what life's storms tout.

Live, learn wait and see

In the silence of the empty room,
Where the mic is off, where shadows loom,
I stand alone, forgotten and lost,
No longer the savior, at a great cost.

I've journeyed far, but lost my way,
Wearing a mask, day by day,
Tears like rivers, unseen by most,
Drowning in sorrows, a heavy ghost.

I walked in shoes I swore I'd shun,
A perfect fit, but soon undone,
Feeding hope, a task I failed,
Lost in a mirror, pale and veiled.

Drinking water to hide the pain,
A clear facade, a fragile chain,
Silenced by doubt, for years I strayed,
Lost in the dark, where fears paraded.

No more fake smiles, no more lies,
Just silent texts, where my truth lies,
An embarrassment, a silent plea,
To find myself, to break free.

Stepping away, letting go of control,
To find what's true, to make me whole,
Embracing the journey, the unknown fate,
Learning to accept, to appreciate.

Life's race is mine, and mine alone,
A path to walk, a truth to own,
With tools in hand, and lessons learned,
I'll find my way, my spirit yearned.

Not everyone will walk beside,
But in the end, I'll stand with pride,
For life can't be rushed or forced to be,
In its vastness, I'll find me.

Silence - a journey within

In the symphony of chaos, silence sings,
A soothing balm for wounded wings.
When doubts and fears ignite the fire,
Retreat to quiet, let your soul aspire.

Like a gentle shade on a scorching day,
Silence shields you from the blinding fray.
When timelines taunt and goals seem far,
In the stillness, find your guiding star.

Amidst the clamor of others' voices loud,
In silence, find your inner shroud.
Reflect, observe, let wisdom bloom,
In the hush, dispel the gloom.

A healing elixir for a weary mind,
Silence whispers truths you'll find.
When sickness grips and shadows loom,
In the quiet, let your spirit resume.

Embrace the silence, let it be your guide,
In its depths, your strength will abide.
When the world's too much, and doubts hold
sway,
Find solace in the silence, let it lead the way.

Mama knows best

In the journey of life, a mother's wisdom
weaves,
Each thread a lesson, each word a guide she
leaves.
"I wasn't born yesterday," she softly said,
Her words a map for life, in paths we tread.

Navigating highways, avoiding treacherous
shorts,
The long waits she endured, teaching life's
retorts.
Her love, a beacon, a steady guiding light,
To shield us from the darkness, to lead us
through the night.

A child's understanding evolves with time,
Through trials and errors, through reason and
rhyme.
A mother's goal, to spare us pain and strife,
To keep us from the flaws that mar our life.

Even when we stray, lose our way in the night,
She's there to guide us back into the light.
Her love knows no bounds, no limits in sight,
A form of protection, a shield so bright.

As we grow, we believe our way is the key,
But humility blooms when we finally see,
To say those words, "You were right, Mom,"
A testament of love, a harmonious psalm.

Warrior

In the quiet depths of night, she stands,
A beacon of strength in shadow's trance,
Though burdened by the weight of unseen
chains,
Her spirit flickers, but never wanes.

Unseen battles etched upon her face,
Yet she carries on with quiet grace,
Strength defined by more than just a show,
In her silence, a resilience starts to grow.

Through storms of doubt and raging fears,
She weathers on, despite the tears,
For in her heart a fire burns,
A beacon in the darkest night.

Her struggles known to only a few,
Yet in her eyes, a truth shines through,
A strength that's born from depths within,
A quiet force that's bound to win.

So here's to the women strong and true,
Who face each day with courage anew,
Though weary hearts may sometimes ache,
Their strength and grace will never break.

Cycles

We twirl with nature's grace,
Where raindrops fall like notes, a cleansing embrace.
They wash away the pain, the sorrow, the ache,
A ritual of healing, a soulful lake.

Air serenades our journey, a melody divine,
A zephyr of change, a rhythm so fine.
We soar on winds of destiny, on paths unknown we tread,
Navigating life's sonata, where dreams are fed.

Fire pirouettes fiercely, a ballet of light,
Consuming the old, igniting our flight.
From the ashes, rebirth blooms,
In the flames of renewal, our spirit looms.

Earth is our stage, full of color,
Where experiences unite, painting our muse.
We harmonize the elements, in life's grand score,
Crafting joy from chaos, forevermore.

In this celestial ballad, we find our tune,
Nature's melody guiding, under the moon.
Through rain, air, fire, and earth's tender caress,
We embrace the elements, in life's sweet progress.

Because

Listen to the soul's sweet sonnet, a melody pure
and bright,
Unleashing boundless potential, a masterpiece in
flight.
Soar upon wings of valor, past the ethereal sky,
In the hallowed halls of self-belief, you become
a legend high.
There is only one you!

Ace the test.

Through trials and tests, it will prevail,
A timeless truth that will never fail.
For in the end, when all is said and done,
Goodness shines bright, like the morning sun.

www.ingramcontent.com/pod-product-compliance
Lightning Source LLC
LaVergne TN
LVHW010953200726
843509LV00013B/2392